LIVING GREEN

CLOTHING

Information and projects to help you live more sustainably

MACMILLAN LIBRARY

Helen Whittaker

First published in 2011 by
MACMILLAN EDUCATION AUSTRALIA PTY LTD
15–19 Claremont Street, South Yarra 3141

Visit our website at www.macmillan.com.au or go directly to www.macmillanlibrary.com.au

Associated companies and representatives throughout the world.

National Library of Australia Cataloguing-in-Publication entry

Whittaker, Helen.
    Clothing / Helen Whittaker.
    ISBN: 978 1 4202 8162 0 (hbk.)
    Whittaker, Helen. Living green.
    Includes index.
    For primary school age.
    Clothing and dress – Juvenile literature.
646.34

Publisher: Carmel Heron
Commissioning Editor: Niki Horin
Managing Editor: Vanessa Lanaway
Editor: Georgina Garner
Proofreader: Helena Newton
Designer: Julie Thompson
Page layout: Julie Thompson
Photo researcher: Claire Armstrong (management: Debbie Gallagher)
Illustrators: Nives Porcellato and Andrew Craig (**11**); Cat MacInnes (all other illustrations)
Production Controller: Vanessa Johnson

Printed in China

Acknowledgements
The author and publisher are grateful to the following for permission to reproduce copyright material:

Front cover photograph: Girl choosing clothes courtesy of Getty Images/Digital Vision. Front and back
cover illustrations by Cat MacInnes.

Photographs courtesy of: Corbis/Ocean, **22** (bottom), /Jose Luis Pelaez, Inc, **5**, /Ariel Skelley, **20**; Getty
Images/Digital Vision, **16**, /Ryan McVay, **18** (left); iStockphoto.com/Greg da Silva, **31**, /Bernad Gavril, **3**,
24 (right), /halfshag, **25** (right), /JazzIRT, **12**, /Juanmonino, **15** (left), /mikapp, **7** (bottom left), /thelinke, **9**
(bottom), /Jason Todd, **26**; Shutterstock, **10**, /1000 Words, **7** (top), /aborisov, **18** (right), /Akaiser,
(environment icons, throughout), /Petrenko Andriy, **17**, /Noam Armonn, **6** (top), **11** (bottom), /Katrina
Brown, **4**, **32**, Ivan Cholakov Gostock-dot-net, **11** (aeroplane), /Lucian Coman, **8** (right), /cristi180884, **23**,
/Elena Elisseeva, **14** (top), /Faraways, **11** (top), /BW Folsom, **25** (left), /Luisa Fernanda Gonzalez, **8** (left), /
gsmad, **30** (middle), /Péter Gudella, **11** (truck), /Kayros Studio, **22** (top), /Laenz, (eco icons, throughout), /
mmaxer, **30** (top), /Monkey Business Images, **28** (left), /Thomas M Perkins, **14** (bottom), /Photosani, **24**
(left), /PrairieEyes, **9** (top), **15** (right), /Rafael Ramirez Lee, **11** (ship), /sokolovsky, **13**, /Kenneth Sponsler,
11 (train), /Steyno&Stitch, **29**, /vale_t, **6** (bottom), /Stephen VanHorn, **28** (right), /Ye, (recycle logos,
throughout), /Yellowj, **7** (bottom right), /Jin Young Lee, **30** (bottom).

Please note
At the time of printing, the Internet addresses appearing in this book were correct. Owing to the dynamic
nature of the Internet, however, we cannot guarantee that all these addresses will remain correct.

CONTENTS

Transform a toothbrush into wearable art! >> *page 24*

Glossary words
When a word is printed in **bold**, you can look up its meaning in the Glossary on page 31.

Put more green in your clean! >> *page 28*

LIVING GREEN

Living green means choosing to care for the **environment** by living in a sustainable way.

Living SUSTAINABLY

Living sustainably means living in a way that protects Earth. Someone who lives sustainably avoids damaging the environment so that Earth can continue to provide a home for people in the future. They do not waste natural resources, so that in the future there will still be enough resources for people to use.

You and your friends can change your habits and behaviour to help Earth. Living green makes sense!

WHAT IS AN ENVIRONMENTAL FOOTPRINT?

A person's environmental footprint describes how much damage that person does to the environment and how quickly they use up Earth's resources. A person who protects the environment and does not waste resources has a light environmental footprint. A person who pollutes the environment and wastes resources has a heavy environmental footprint.

ENVIRONMENTAL IMPACTS of our actions

Human activities use up Earth's **natural resources** and damage the environment. Some natural resources are **renewable**, such as wind and water, and some are **non-renewable**, such as the **fossil fuels** coal and petroleum.

As the world's population grows, humans are using more water, creating water shortages and water **pollution**. We are using more non-renewable resources too, which are usually mined from the earth and then burned, causing **habitat** destruction and air pollution. Humans cannot continue to live and act the way we do now – this way of life is unsustainable.

CLOTHING

The clothes we choose to buy have an impact on the environment. Understanding these environmental effects can help us choose 'greener' clothing and live more sustainably.

How clothing affects the ENVIRONMENT

The clothes you wear affect the environment at every stage of their lives, from when the **fabric** is made to when the clothes are worn and washed. Often, lots of water and chemicals are used to create fabric, and this uses up natural resources and pollutes the environment. The energy needed to **manufacture**, package, transport and clean clothing is often created by burning fossil fuels, which harms the environment and is not sustainable.

>> Where to NEXT?

>> To find out how the production, packaging, transport and cleaning of clothes affect the environment, go to the BACKGROUND BRIEFING section on page 6.

>> To try out fun projects that will help you reduce your environmental footprint, go to the LIVING GREEN PROJECTS section on page 16.

How does buying a COTTON T-SHIRT affect the ENVIRONMENT?

The T-shirt you are wearing may have been made in a factory on another continent, then been shipped to a store in your neighbourhood before finiding a place in your home. The journey of that T-shirt may have had a bad effect on the environment.

Growing the cotton

A lot of water is used to grow cotton, and harmful chemicals are often used.

Making the fabric

Spinning and weaving cotton uses energy. Most electrical energy is generated using fossil fuels. Chemicals used in factories can pollute the environment.

Manufacturing the T-shirt

Sewing machines in clothing factories use energy.

Packaging the T-shirt

Packaging uses up natural resources and may use non-renewable materials.

Transporting the T-shirt to the store

Planes and trucks burn fossil fuels.

Cleaning the T-shirt

Washing clothes uses energy and water, and **detergents** can cause water pollution.

MAKING fabric

Your clothes are made from different **fabrics**, which are woven from fibres. Producing fibres and making them into fabric can damage the **environment** and use up **natural resources**.

The environmental impacts of MAKING FABRIC

Fabric can be made from natural or **artificial fibres**. Artificial fibres are made from **non-renewable resources**, so they are not sustainable. Turning both natural and artificial fibres into fabric uses lots of water and electrical energy. This uses up natural resources. Making fabric also uses **toxic** chemicals that **pollute** and harm the environment.

Natural fibres from cotton bushes are harvested and spun into cotton cloth. Often, growing cotton uses large amounts of water and poisonous chemicals.

*Weaving machines in factories use large amounts of electricity. Most electricity is generated by burning **fossil fuels**.*

NATURAL FIBRES versus ARTIFICIAL FIBRES

Artificial fibres are created in factories using raw materials, such as **petroleum**, which are mined from the ground. Nylon, polyester and acrylic are some artificial fibres. **Natural fibres** are fibres that come from animals or plants, such as wool from sheep and cotton from cotton bushes. The most sustainable types of fabric are made from natural fibres grown without artificial **fertilisers** or **pesticides**, and that are not bleached and are dyed using **non-toxic** dyes.

Producing FIBRES and making FABRIC

This flow chart shows the main processes involved in making fabric, and the impacts they have on the environment.

Making fabric from artificial fibres

Mine the raw materials

- The raw materials come from non-renewable sources.
- Mining uses a lot of energy. It can also destroy **habitats** and create pollution.

Turn the materials into artificial fibres

High temperatures are needed to combine the materials and create artificial fibres. This uses a lot of energy.

Making fabric from natural fibres

Grow plants or raise animals to produce the fibres

- Fertilisers can pollute water sources.
- Pesticides can kill helpful insects.
- **Irrigation** can create water shortages.

Untangle, clean and dry the fibres

A lot of water and energy are used.

Spin the fibres into thread and weave it into cloth

Spinning and weaving machines use energy.

Bleach, dye and finish the cloth

Bleaches, dyes and finishing agents are toxic. They can leak out of the factory, polluting streams and rivers.

MANUFACTURING clothes

After **fabric** is made, it is sent to another factory – sometimes in a different country – where it is made into clothes. **Manufacturing** clothes has its own set of **environmental** impacts.

The environmental impacts of MANUFACTURING CLOTHES

Most clothes are not manufactured sustainably. Fabric often needs to be transported a long way to clothing factories, and the machines in clothing factories use a lot of electricity. Most of this electricity is generated by burning **fossil fuels**, which harms the environment and is not sustainable. The manufactured clothes are given special treatments that use a lot of water and can **pollute** the environment.

Factory workers use electrical sewing machines to sew pieces of fabric together. Most electricity is generated by burning fossil fuels, which has a negative impact on the environment.

Manufacturing clothes in a factory

This flow chart shows the main steps involved in manufacturing clothes.

A designer designs the piece of clothing on a computer.
↓
A machine cuts out pattern pieces.
↓
Spreading machines stack the fabric.
↓
Pattern pieces are fastened to the fabric.

Machines cut out the pieces of fabric.
↓
Sewing machine operators sew the pieces of fabric together.
↓
The clothing is pressed and it is decorated or given any special treatments.
↓
The clothes are checked to make sure they look good and are safe to wear.

TRANSPORTING the fabric to the clothing factory

The factory where the clothes are made may be in a different city, country or even continent to the place where the fabric was manufactured. The trucks, trains, boats or aeroplanes used to transport the fabric run on fuels made from **petroleum**, a fossil fuel.

SPECIAL TREATMENTS for clothes

Clothes are sometimes given special treatments before they leave a factory. Different treatments have different purposes and different environmental impacts.

Special treatments for clothes

Treatment	Purpose	Environmental impact
Washing	To remove dye and lighten the colour	Uses a lot of water
Applying chemicals	To make the clothes: • look worn • feel softer • wrinkle-free • flameproof.	Contributes to water pollution

ECO FACT

Some pieces of clothing are marked with an 'ecolabel', which explains why the manufacturer considers the clothing sustainable. The International Organization for Standardization (ISO) is developing an international labelling system for clothing that is manufactured sustainably.

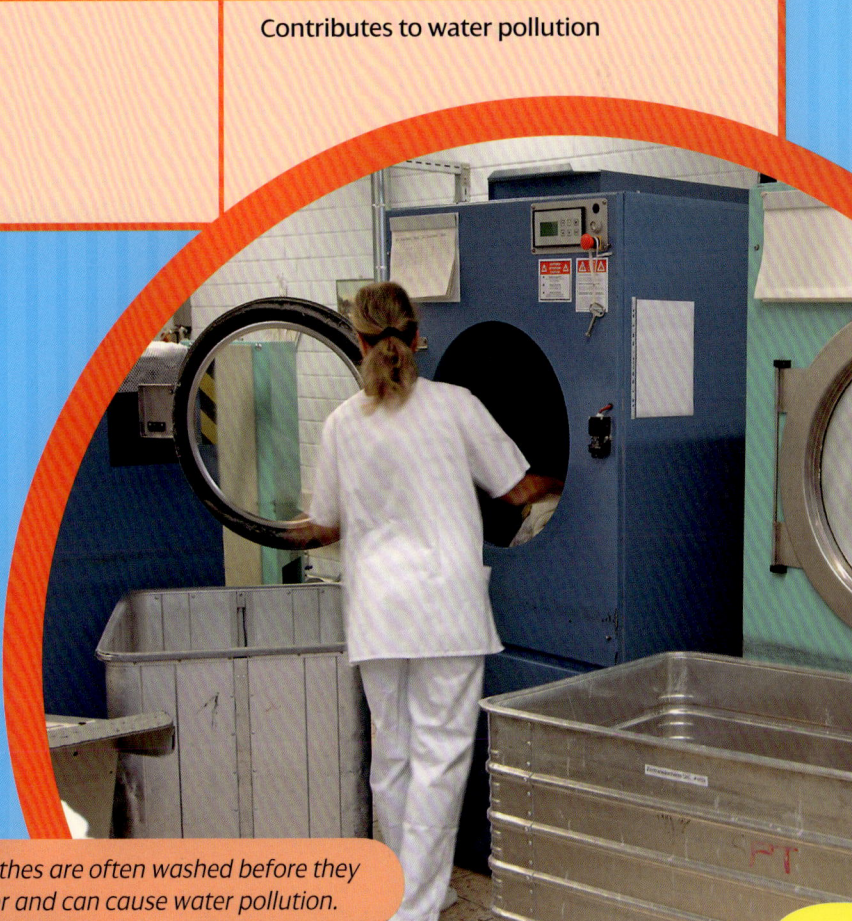

Your clothes are washed before they even get dirty! Clothes are often washed before they leave a factory. Washing the clothes uses lots of water and can cause water pollution.

PACKAGING and TRANSPORTING clothes

Once clothes have been **manufactured**, they are packaged and transported to clothing stores. When you buy clothes in a store, they are often placed into a plastic bag – even more packaging!

Some clothes, come with a lot of packaging. Not all of the packaging can be recycled.

The environmental impacts of PACKAGING and TRANSPORTING CLOTHES

Many clothes are packaged before they are sent to stores to be sold, and they are often packaged in another bag when sold. Packaging wastes **natural resources** and it usually becomes **landfill**.

Clothing manufacturers transport and sell their clothes all over the world. Transporting clothes involves burning a lot of **fossil fuel**, which harms the **environment** and uses up resources.

PACKAGING CLOTHES

Common packaging materials for clothes are cardboard, tissue paper and plastic. In most cases, this packaging is unnecessary. It is a waste of resources and if it is not **recycled**, it contributes to the growing mountain of waste in landfill sites.

ECO FACT

Some plastic clothes packaging is made from PVC (polyvinyl chloride), which is a type of plastic used around the world because it is cheap and long-lasting. Burning waste PVC releases **toxic** gases that can cause health problems for animals and humans.

TRANSPORTING CLOTHES around the world

From the factory, clothes may be taken by truck to a port, where they are loaded onto a container ship. When the ship reaches its destination, the clothes are loaded into trucks, which take the clothes to the stores where they will be sold. Ships and trucks run on fossil fuels, so they use up natural resources. They also release **carbon dioxide**, which is linked to **global warming**. The more carbon dioxide a vehicle produces, the more it harms the environment.

Transport vehicles and the amount of carbon dioxide they release

Transport vehicle	Carbon dioxide (grams) released when carrying 1 tonne of food over 1 kilometre (0.6 mile)
Train 	39–48 grams
Ship 	40–60 grams
Truck 	207–280 grams
Aeroplane 	1160–2150 grams

*This map shows the top six **importers** of clothing and the top six **exporters** of clothing in 2008. Transporting clothing long distances has negative environmental impacts.*

CLEANING clothes

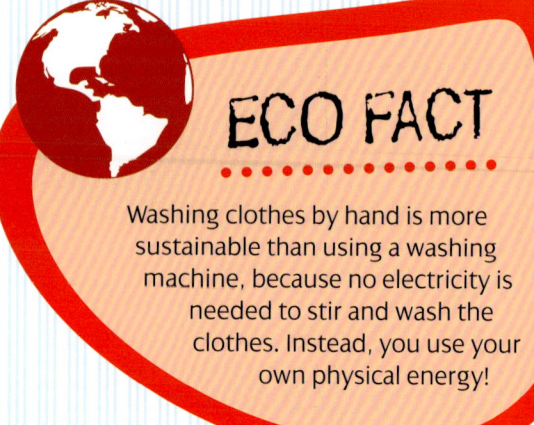

causes pollution

uses water

uses electrical energy

Using a washing machine is an easy way to wash clothes, but it has three major impacts on the environment.

Your clothes have an **environmental** impact even after you have bought them. When you wear your clothes, you get them dirty and they need to be cleaned. Washing and drying clothes can affect the environment in many ways.

The environmental impacts of CLEANING CLOTHES

Washing clothes in a washing machine has an impact on the environment because the machine uses lots of water and electrical energy, and washing **detergents** are rinsed away and can cause **pollution**. Drying clothes in a tumble dryer uses lots of electrical energy, and dry-cleaning uses chemicals that harm the environment.

WASHING CLOTHES in a washing machine

Washing machines have three major impacts on the environment.

- Washing machines use up to 100 litres (26 gallons) of water per load. In many parts of the world, water is in short supply and washing machines use up this **natural resource**.
- The machines use electrical energy to heat the water and rotate the drum. Most electricity is generated by burning **fossil fuels**, which harms the environment and is not sustainable.
- Most laundry detergents contain chemicals made from **petroleum**. They are rinsed down the drain and eventually reach rivers and the sea. The chemicals they contain are harmful to plants and animals.

ECO FACT

Washing clothes by hand is more sustainable than using a washing machine, because no electricity is needed to stir and wash the clothes. Instead, you use your own physical energy!

DRYING CLOTHES

Tumble dryers are a popular way of drying clothes, but they use a lot of electrical energy. The most sustainable way to dry clothes is to hang them outside on a line.

ECO FACT

Different electrical appliances have different power ratings, which are measured in watts (W) or kilowatts (kW). One kilowatt hour (1 kWh) is the amount of energy that an appliance with a power of 1 kilowatt uses during 1 hour. The more energy an appliance uses, the greater its environmental impact.

Electrical energy needed to dry one load of laundry in different ways

Drying method		Electrical energy used (kilowatt hours)
Tumble drying	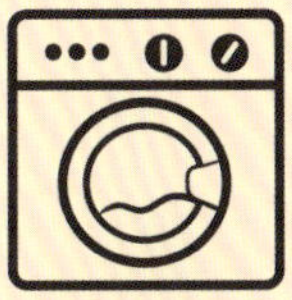	4.9 kWh
Dehumidifier		2.1 kWh
Heated drying rack	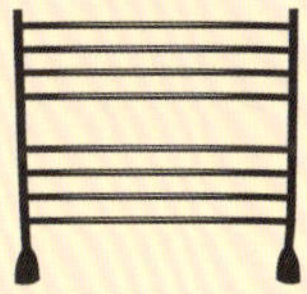	1.5 kWh
Line drying		0 kWh

Drying a load of laundry on a line uses no electrical energy, so it is a sustainable choice.

DRY-CLEANING

Dry-cleaning uses harmful chemicals. Small amounts of these chemicals are left behind on clothes that have been dry-cleaned, and breathing them in can cause health problems. Waste materials from dry-cleaning, such as plastic hangers and coverings, become **landfill**.

What can YOU do?

Making green choices when buying clothes can help protect Earth and our future.

You can do many things to reduce the **environmental** impact of the clothes you wear. Start with making sustainable choices when you buy and clean clothes.

Green tips for BUYING CLOTHES

Choose clothes that:

✔ are made from **natural fibres** that were grown without **pesticides** and **fertilisers** or that are made from **recycled** materials

✔ have little or no packaging

✔ are second-hand or 'vintage'

✔ were made in the country where you live.

Avoid clothes that:

✘ are poorly made and will wear out quickly

✘ need to be dry-cleaned

✘ cannot be washed in cold water.

Green tips for CLEANING CLOTHES

To save both water and energy:

✔ wait until you have a full load before putting on the washing machine.

To save energy:

✔ wash your clothes on the cold temperature setting

✔ hang your clothes outside to dry.

To reduce **pollution**:

✔ use environmentally friendly laundry **detergent**.

Local charity shops are a great way of disposing of unwanted clothes and getting new clothes. Shopping for one-of-a-kind clothing is lots of fun, too!

Green tips for CLOTHES YOU ALREADY OWN

✔ Refashion the clothes you already have.

✔ Take old clothes to a local charity shop or recycling depot.

✔ Organise a clothing 'swap shop' with friends.

Living Green ratings and Green tips

Pages 16–29 are filled with fun projects that will help you reuse and refashion the clothes in your wardrobe and protect Earth from waste and pollution.

Each project is given its own Living Green star rating out of five stars, which is a measurement of how much the project lightens your environmental footprint.

Some projects give Green Tips telling you how you can improve the project's Living Green rating even more.

Green tip

To improve the Living Green rating, make the strap from an old belt or a bicycle inner tube.

On each project spread, look for a project's Living Green rating. Five stars is the highest – and greenest – rating!

Living Green rating

⭐⭐⭐⭐

• Reduces the need to buy new jewellery, so less environmental impact
• Reduces **landfill**, because the old toothbrush is not thrown out as waste

A three-star project might teach you about an issue and explain how you are wasting **natural resources** or causing pollution.	A four-star project might show one or two ways to reduce waste or pollution.	A five-star project might help you reduce waste and pollution and actively protect the environment in many different ways.

MAKE OVER a T-shirt

Give new life to old clothes

Giving new life to old clothes is more sustainable than buying new clothes. When your favourite printed T-shirt becomes holey, stained or out of shape, don't throw it out! Use it to update a plain, boring T-shirt.

Living Green rating

⭐ ⭐ ⭐ ⭐

- Reduces the need to buy new clothes, so less **environmental** impact
- Reduces **landfill**, because the old T-shirt is not thrown out as waste

What you need

- Favourite T-shirt
- Plain T-shirt
- Pinking shears or scissors
- Iron-on interfacing
- Iron
- Needle
- Thread
- Sewing pins

What to do

1. Choose a large piece of the printed T-shirt that is not stained or holey. Cut out a piece using pinking shears or scissors.

2. Pin this large patch to the iron-on interfacing. Make sure the sticky side of the interfacing is against the back of the patch.

3. Cut around the edges of the patch.

Don't always buy new clothes. Reuse your old or worn-out clothes and make one-of-a-kind outfits!

Green tip

Make sure that the fabric patch can be washed in the same type of wash cycle as the T-shirt you are adding it to. You don't want the patch to shrink in the wash.

4. Iron the interfacing to the patch, and then remove the pins. The interfacing will stop the patch from fraying.

Only use an iron under adult supervision. ⚠

5. Pin the patch to the front of the other T-shirt.

6. Hand sew the patch to the T-shirt.

7. Remove the pins and try on your new T-shirt!

REUSING old clothes

Repairing, altering and making over your clothes will mean that your clothes last for much longer – and you'll have some one-of-a-kind items.

- Mend rips or holes by covering them with a patch.
- If your pant legs become too short, add fabric to make them longer or turn them into shorts.
- Use old clothes to make a new item – for example, make a supporter's flag from an old sports shirt.
- Give old clothing a new look by dyeing it (see pages 20–23), adding a design using **non-toxic** fabric paints, sewing on ribbons or sequins, or replacing the buttons.

Upgrade to ARM WARMERS

Transform an old jumper into new arm warmers

One way to reduce the number of new clothes you need to buy is to transform old clothes into new ones. Make your own original arm warmers from an old, holey jumper.

Living Green rating

★ ★ ★ ★ ★

- Reduces the need to buy new clothes, so less **environmental** impact
- Reduces **landfill**, because the old jumper is not thrown out as waste
- Reduces the need for electrical heating, because the arm warmers keep your arms and hands warm

What you need

- Old woollen jumper
- Measuring tape or ruler
- Pen
- Paper
- Needle
- Thread
- Scissors

What to do

1. Measure the distance from your elbow to your knuckles. Add 1.5 centimetres (0.6 inch) and then write the measurement down.

2. Cut both sleeves off the jumper.

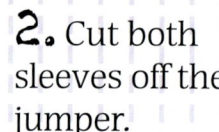

Find a holey, woollen jumper and turn it into stylish arm warmers.

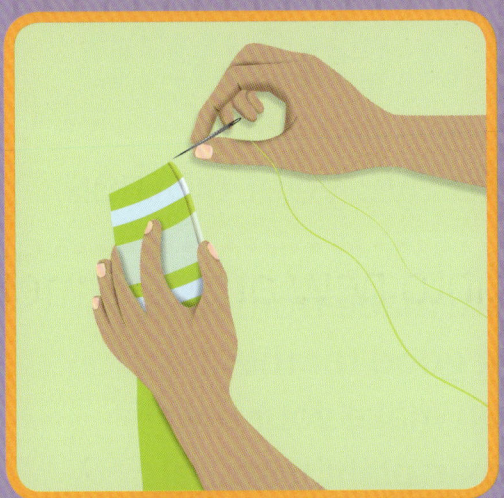

3. Starting from the cuff of one sleeve, measure the distance that you recorded in step 1. Mark this with a pin and then cut the sleeve here.

4. Turn the sleeve inside out. At the edge you just cut, fold the material over 0.5 centimetres (0.2 inch) and then fold it again another 1 centimetre (0.4 inch). Pin the edge.

5. Hand sew this hem.

6. Turn the arm warmer rightside out. Try it on and decide where you would like your thumb hole. Mark this place with a pin.

7. Use the scissors to cut a small slit at the place you marked.

8. Turn the arm warmer inside out. Sew around the edges of the thumb hole so that it won't fray.

9. Repeat steps 3–8 to make the second arm warmer.

Green tip

You could also make arm warmers from old striped socks that have holes in their toes.

DYEING for a change

Use plants and food to dye your clothes

Most shop-bought dyes are made from **toxic** chemicals, so they are not good for the **environment**. But you can make your own natural dyes from **non-toxic** plant materials.

Living Green rating
★ ★ ★ ★

• Reduces the need to buy new clothes, so less environmental impact
• Uses natural dyes, so no toxic chemicals are released to **pollute** the water system

What you need

• Piece of cotton clothing, such as a singlet
• Plant materials (see table below)
• Large saucepan
• Vinegar
• Salt
• Measuring jug
• Mixing bowl
• Knife
• Chopping board
• Rubber gloves

What to do

1. First, you need to make a special solution that will prepare the **fabric** so that the dye works well. For most plant materials, mix 1 part vinegar with 4 parts cold water. If using berries, mix 1 part salt with 16 parts cold water. Use the measuring jug and mix in a bowl.

2. Half-fill the saucepan with the mixture, and put the singlet into the pan.

Plant materials that can be used as dyes

Colour of dye	Plant materials
Pink or red	Strawberries, cherries, raspberries
Orange	Carrots, lilac twigs, onion skins
Yellow	Turmeric, marigolds, dandelions
Green	Spinach leaves, lilac flowers, snapdragons
Blue or purple	Red cabbage, blackberries, blueberries
Brown	Tea bags, coffee grounds, dandelion roots

Look in your garden or kitchen for plant materials that can be used to make natural dyes.

3. Place the saucepan on the stovetop and simmer for one hour.

Only use the stovetop under adult supervision.

4. Take the saucepan off the heat and leave to cool.

5. Empty the saucepan and rinse the singlet in cold water.

6. Chop up the plant material.

7. Place the plant material in the saucepan. Add twice the volume of cold water as there is plant material.

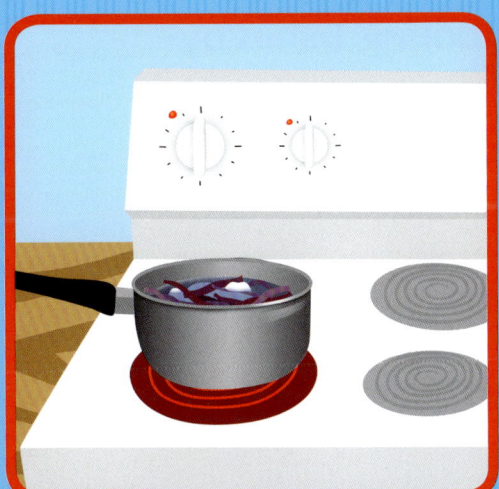

8. Place the singlet in the saucepan. Simmer on the stovetop until you get the right colour. Remember, the colour will lighten as the singlet dries.

9. Remove the saucepan from the heat and leave to cool.

10. Wearing rubber gloves, remove the singlet from the pan.

11. Rinse the singlet in cold water, then hang on the line to dry.

Green tip

For the best results, dye white or light-coloured clothes made from **natural fibres**.

Colour
TRANSFORMATION

Transform an old T-shirt by dyeing it

Once you know how to make natural dyes (see pages 20–21), you can start to experiment with colour. Transform an old, boring T-shirt by adding a colourful pattern.

What you need

• White cotton T-shirt
• Plant materials to make the dye (see page 20)
• Large saucepan
• Vinegar
• Salt
• Measuring jug
• Mixing bowl
• Knife
• Chopping board
• Rubber gloves
• Rubber bands or string

What to do

1. Follow steps 1–7 on pages 20–21.

2. Fold and tie the T-shirt to create the pattern you want (see table on page 23).

3. Follow steps 8–11 on page 21. Untie the T-shirt before rinsing it in step 11.

You can use natural dyes to create different patterns and effects.

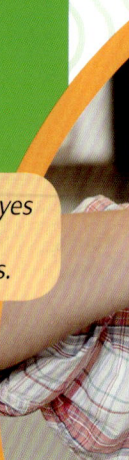

How to create different patterns

Pattern	What to do	Result
Marbled Crumple the T-shirt and tie it many times to get this effect.		
Spiral Swirl the T-shirt and tie it four times to get this effect.		
Stripes Roll the T-shirt and tie up the roll to create stripes.		

EXPERIMENT more

Experiment more with colour and **fabrics**. Try various ways of folding, twisting and pinching the fabric, and place the rubber bands or string in different places. Try dyeing multicoloured fabrics or cotton clothing that has stitching made from **artificial fibres**.

Recycled WRISTBAND

Turn a toothbrush into a fashion statement!

Most store-bought jewellery is not **manufactured** sustainably. By turning an old toothbrush into a colourful wristband, you'll reduce your **environmental** impact – and no one else will have your style!

Living Green rating

★★★★

- Reduces the need to buy new jewellery, so less environmental impact
- Reduces **landfill**, because the old toothbrush is not thrown out as waste

What you need

- An old toothbrush
- Tweezers
- Tongs
- Bowl
- Mug
- Oven gloves
- Tea towel
- 2 cups boiling water
- 1 cup cold water

What to do

1. Use the tweezers to remove the bristles from the toothbrush.

2. Pour the boiling water into the bowl.

3. Use the tongs to put the toothbrush into the bowl of boiling water. Leave for five minutes.

4. Use the tongs to remove the toothbrush from the bowl. Place it on a tea towel.

Take care! Boiling water can burn you! ⚠️

5. Wearing the oven gloves, bend the toothbrush into a wristband shape.

Create one-of-a-kind jewellery using your old, scruffy toothbrush!

6. Put the bent toothbrush into the mug. The sides of the mug will stop the toothbrush from uncurling as it cools.

7. Pour the cold water into the mug. Leave the toothbrush to cool for a few minutes.

8. Wear your wristband as it is or decorate it using one of the ideas below.

DECORATING your wristband

Decorate your wristband by:
- using a metallic marker pen to add your name or the name of a sports team you support
- gluing on sequins, glitter or shiny paper
- tying on old beads using thin thread.

Green tip

Make different kinds of wristbands using these waste materials:
- odd buttons threaded onto sewing thread
- old shoelaces
- scraps of ribbon
- safety pins joined together.

Brand-new BACKPACK

Refashion a T-shirt into a backpack

One way to live more sustainably is by reusing old clothes instead of throwing them away. For this project, you can reuse an old T-shirt to make a stylish backpack that looks as good as new.

Living Green rating

★ ★ ★ ★ ★

- Reduces the need to buy a new bag, so less **environmental** impact
- If shopping, reduces the need to use a plastic bag, so less environmental impact
- Reduces **landfill**, because the old T-shirt is not thrown out as waste

What you need

- Old T-shirt
- Scissors
- Sewing machine
- Needle
- Thread
- Sewing pins
- About 50 centimetres (1.6 feet) of strap
- About 80 centimetres (2.6 feet) of cord
- Safety pin

What to do

1. Turn the T-shirt inside out and lay it flat.

2. Cut off both sleeves.

3. Cut the neck off in a straight line.

4. In one of the cut corners, pin and hand sew the end of the strap to the top layer of the T-shirt.

5. Tuck the strap between the two layers of T-shirt. Keep the strap flat and untwisted.

You can use a little imagination and a sewing machine to turn a T-shirt into a new backpack.

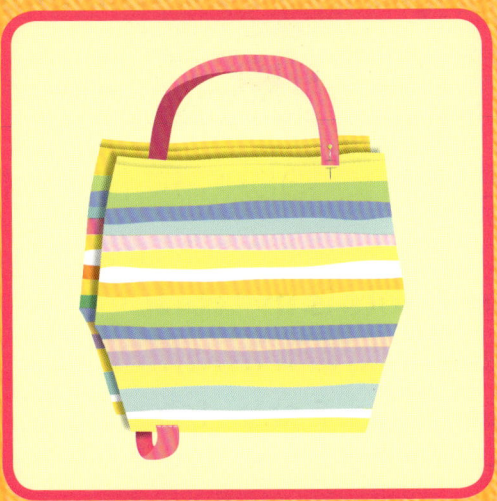

6. Pin the other end of the strap to the opposite corner. Again, pin it to the top layer of the T-shirt.

7. Hand sew the strap to the T-shirt.

8. Pin together the three cut sides of the T-shirt. Sew around the sides using the sewing machine. Do this twice.

Ask an adult for help with the sewing machine. !

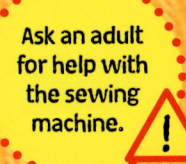

9. Turn the T-shirt right side out.

10. At the top of the backpack, roll the hem between your fingers to separate the two layers. Cut two small slits in the hem, about 2 centimetres (0.75 inch) apart.

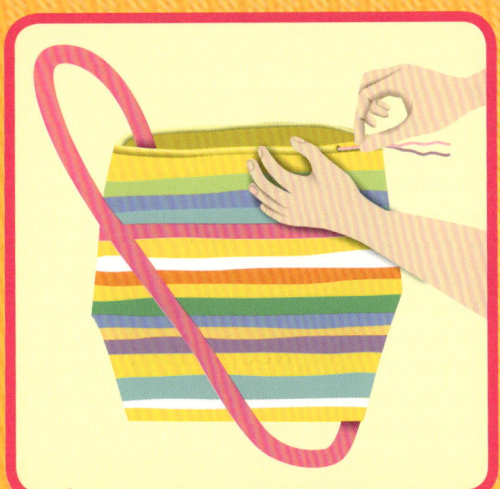

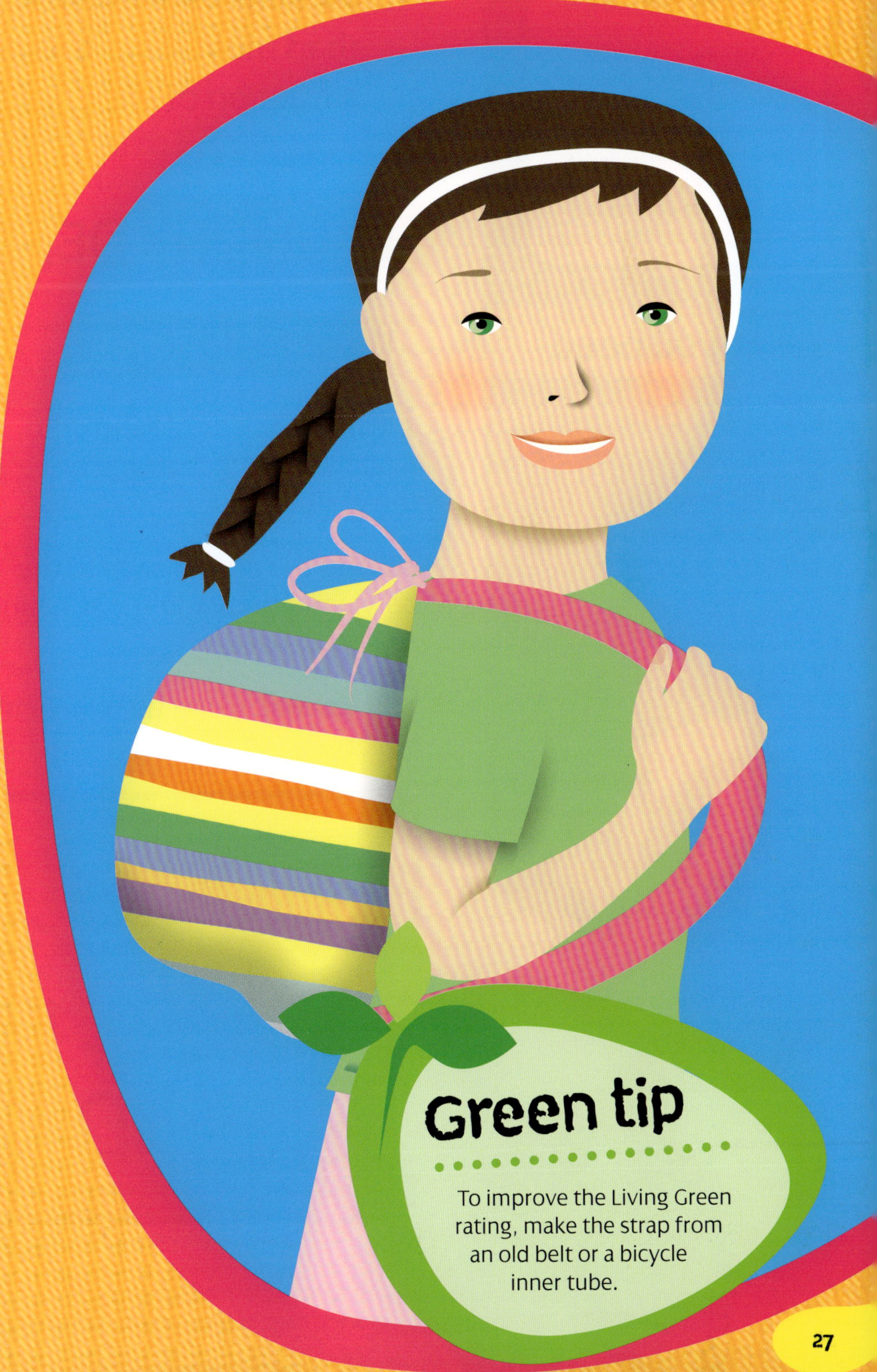

11. Attach a safety pin to one end of the cord and thread the pin and the cord through the hem. Remove the safety pin and tie a large knot in each end of the cord.

12. Try out your new backpack!

Green tip

To improve the Living Green rating, make the strap from an old belt or a bicycle inner tube.

Living Green PROJECTS

GREEN clean

Make your own detergent and fabric softener

Home-made laundry **detergents** and **fabric** softeners are much kinder to the **environment** than most shop-bought versions. They also cost a fraction of the price and are easy to make!

Living Green rating
★ ★ ★ ★

• Reduces the need to buy detergent and fabric softener, so less environmental impact
• Uses natural ingredients, so no **toxic** chemicals are released to **pollute** the water system

LAUNDRY DETERGENT

What you need

• Bar of laundry soap
• 1 cup washing soda
• 1 cup borax
• Large bowl
• Wooden spoon
• Cheese grater
• Plate
• Airtight container

What to do

1. Grate the bar of soap onto a plate. Use the fine side of the grater.

2. Add the grated soap to the bowl, and then add the washing soda and borax.

3. Mix well, using the wooden spoon.

4. Put the detergent in an airtight container.

5. Use 2 tablespoons per load of laundry.

Keep your clothes fresh, clean and good for the environment by washing them in home-made detergent.

FABRIC SOFTENER

What you need

- 4 cups water
- 2 cups white vinegar
- 2 cups **baking soda**
- Large bowl
- Wooden spoon
- Airtight container

What to do

1. Pour the water and vinegar into the bowl.

2. Add the baking soda a little at a time. The mixture will fizz.

3. Stir well.

4. Store in an airtight container.

5. Shake the mixture and add ¼ cup to your washing machine for the final rinse.

Label your containers of detergent and fabric softener and keep them out of the reach of babies and young children.

Green tip

To make your clothes smell fresh, add two or three drops of essential oil to your home-made fabric softener. Oils such as lavender or eucalyptus would work well.

FIND OUT MORE
about living green

The Internet is a great way of finding out more about the **environmental** impact of clothes and what you can do to make more sustainable clothing choices.

USEFUL websites

Visit these useful websites:

http://www.wikihow.com/Recycle-Your-Socks
This page has lots of fun ideas for reusing old socks.

http://diyfashion.about.com/od/recycledprojects/tp/Recycle-Your-Clothes.htm
This page suggests various ways of turning old clothes into new fashion items.

http://unep.org/tunza/children
This website from the United Nations has downloadable fact sheets about environmental issues, tips for living more sustainably and competitions you can enter.

SEARCHING for information

Here are some search terms you might use to find out more information about clothing and sustainability:
• environmental impact of clothing
• cotton and **pesticides**
• organic cotton
• **recycled fabric**
• wardrobe refashion.

GLOSSARY

artificial fibres fibres that are made by humans and do not come directly from nature

baking soda white, powdery chemical compound used for cooking and cleaning; also called sodium bicarbonate or bicarb soda

carbon dioxide a greenhouse gas that is released when fossil fuels are burned, such as when coal is burned to make electricity

detergents liquid or powder cleaning materials that clean away dirt and oil

environment the natural world, including plants, animals, land, rivers and seas

exporters countries that send products to another country for sale

fabric cloth produced by weaving or knitting fibres together

fertilisers substances added to the soil to help crops grow better

fossil fuels coal, oil and natural gas, which are natural resources that are formed from the remains of dead plants and animals, deep under Earth's surface, over millions of years

global warming process by which Earth's average temperature is getting warmer

habitat place where plants, animals and other living things live

importers countries that bring in products from another country

irrigation the supplying of water to a dry area to help crops grow

landfill rubbish that is buried and covered with soil at tips or dumps

manufacture make from raw materials into a product for people to buy and use

natural fibres fibres from plants and animals, such as cotton and wool, which can be spun and woven into cloth

natural resources natural materials that can be used by humans, such as wood, metal, coal and water

non-renewable resources natural resources that cannot be easily replaced, such as coal, oil and natural gas, which take millions of years to replace

non-toxic not poisonous to living things

pesticides poisonous chemicals used to kill pests, such as insects, fungi and weeds, to prevent them from damaging crops

petroleum a liquid found in rocks, formed from the remains of plants and animals that lived millions of years ago; also known as oil or crude oil

pollution damaging substances, especially chemicals or waste products, that harm the environment

recycled having treated the materials contained in a product so that they can be used again

renewable resources natural resources that will never run out, such as the wind, or that can easily be replaced, such as wood

toxic poisonous to living things

INDEX